Candy Cane
· Cookbook ·

D0115073

Compiled by Patricia Lutherbeck in association with Snapdragon Group℠, Tulsa, OK

Print ISBN 978-1-61626-832-9

eBook Editions:
Adobe Digital Edition (.epub) 978-1-62029-068-2
Kindle and MobiPocket Edition (.prc) 978-1-62029-069-9

Published by Barbour Publishing, Inc., P.O. Box 719, Uhrichsville, Ohio 44683, www.barbourbooks.com

Our mission is to publish and distribute inspirational products offering exceptional value and biblical encouragement to the masses.

ecpa Member of the
Evangelical Christian
Publishers Association

Printed in the United States of America.

Taste of Christmas

Candy Cane
• Cookbook •

& Inspiration for the Season

BARBOUR
PUBLISHING

Candy canes—
all crunchy and sweet.
They are a favorite
Christmassy treat!

Contents

The candy cane began as a long, straight, white, sugar candy stick. But through the years, it has become much more. Legend has it that a German choirmaster, hoping to quiet noisy children during the nativity ceremony, bent the ends into the shape of a shepherd's staff, representing the shepherds who came to visit the infant Jesus. By 1900, candy canes came with red stripes and peppermint flavoring. Today you can find them in many sizes, colors, and flavors.

This Christmas cookbook is a celebration of the candy cane. They have been incorporated into every recipe from cookies to pies and cakes, beverages, desserts, and much more, adding a little more festivity to your Christmas celebrations.

Cookies and Bars

Therefore the Lord himself shall give you a sign;
Behold, a virgin shall conceive, and bear a son,
and shall call his name Immanuel.
Isaiah 7:14

Chocolate Mint Pecan Crisps

1 cup light brown sugar, packed
½ cup butter, softened
12 large peppermint candy canes, finely crushed
1 egg
1 teaspoon vanilla
1½ cups flour
1 cup pecans, chopped
⅓ cup unsweetened cocoa powder
½ teaspoon baking soda
1 cup flaked coconut

Beat brown sugar, butter, and crushed candy canes until light and fluffy. Beat in egg and vanilla. Combine flour, pecans, cocoa, and baking soda. Stir into creamed mixture to form stiff dough. Sprinkle coconut on work surface. Divide dough into 4 parts. Shape each part into a roll about 1½ inches in diameter. Roll in coconut until thickly coated. Wrap in plastic wrap and refrigerate at least 1 hour. Cut rolls into ⅛-inch slices; place on ungreased cookie sheets. Bake at 350 degrees for 10 to 13 minutes or until firm. Cool on wire racks.

Yield: 5 dozen cookies.

Chocolate Peppermint Pinwheels

1 cup shortening
1½ cups sugar
8 large peppermint
 candy canes,
 finely crushed

2 eggs
2 tablespoons milk
¼ teaspoon peppermint
 extract
2½ cups flour
½ teaspoon salt

½ teaspoon baking
 powder
2 (1 ounce) squares
 unsweetened
 chocolate, melted

Cream together shortening, sugar, and crushed candy canes until light and fluffy. Add eggs, milk, and extract. Mix well. Combine flour, salt, and baking powder and gradually add to creamed mixture. Divide dough in half. Add chocolate to one portion. Mix well. Roll each portion between waxed paper into 16 x 7-inch rectangle, about ¼-inch thick. Remove top sheet of waxed paper; place plain dough over chocolate dough. Roll up, starting with long side. Wrap in plastic wrap; refrigerate for 2 hours. Cut into ¼-inch slices. Place 2 inches apart on greased cookie sheets. Bake at 375 degrees for 8 to 10 minutes.

Yield: 4 dozen cookies.

Peppermint Stars

1 cup butter, softened
1¾ cups sugar
12 large peppermint
    candy canes,
    finely crushed

2 eggs
2¾ cups flour
3 large peppermint
    candy canes,
    finely crushed

Cream together butter, sugar, and crushed candy canes until light and
fluffy. Add eggs, one at a time, beating well after each. Gradually
add flour to creamed mixture. Cover and refrigerate for 1 hour.
On lightly floured surface, roll out to ¼-inch thickness. Cut
with 2½-inch star-shaped cookie cutter dipped in flour.
Place 1 inch apart on ungreased cookie sheets.
Bake at 350 degrees for 15 to 18 minutes.
Immediately sprinkle with crushed candy canes.

Yield: 5 dozen cookies.

Peppermint Mocha Truffle Cookies

½ cup butter, cubed	¾ cup sugar	⅛ teaspoon peppermint
1½ cups semisweet	¾ cup brown sugar,	extract
chocolate chips,	packed	2 cups flour
divided	12 large peppermint	⅓ cup baking cocoa
3 teaspoons instant	candy canes,	½ teaspoon baking
coffee granules	finely crushed	powder
2 eggs	2 teaspoons vanilla	¼ teaspoon salt

Over low heat, melt butter and ½ cup chocolate chips. Remove from heat
and stir until smooth. Stir in coffee granules. Cool for 5 minutes. Stir in eggs,
sugars, crushed candy canes, vanilla, and peppermint extract. Combine
flour, cocoa, baking powder, and salt and fold into chocolate mixture with
remaining chocolate chips. Drop by teaspoonfuls 2 inches apart onto
greased cookie sheets. Bake at 350 degrees for 9 to 11
minutes or until tops are slightly dry and cracked.
Cool for 1 minute.

Yield: 5 dozen cookies.

Peppermint Brownie Drops

⅓ cup butter, softened
¾ cup sugar
10 large peppermint candy canes, finely crushed
⅓ cup light corn syrup

1 egg
3 (1 ounce) squares unsweetened chocolate, melted
1 teaspoon vanilla
1 ⅔ cups flour

½ teaspoon baking powder
¼ teaspoon salt
½ cup walnuts, chopped

Cream together butter, sugar, and crushed candy canes until light and fluffy. Add corn syrup and egg. Beat well. Stir in chocolate and vanilla. Combine flour, baking powder, and salt and add to chocolate mixture. Beat well. Stir in walnuts. Drop by teaspoonfuls 2 inches apart onto greased cookie sheets. Bake at 350 degrees for 10 to 12 minutes or until edges are firm.

Yield: 2 dozen cookies.

Peppermint Sandwich Cookies

1 (16 ounce) can vanilla frosting	72 round butter-flavored crackers
10 large peppermint candy canes, finely crushed	1 pound dark chocolate candy coating, coarsely chopped

Combine frosting and crushed candy canes. Spread over half of crackers; top with remaining crackers. Heat candy coating in microwave, stirring frequently, until smooth. Dip cookies in coating. Place on chilled cookie sheet covered with waxed paper until set.

Yield: 3 dozen cookies.

Ricotta Cheese Peppermint Cookies

2 cups sugar
12 large peppermint
candy canes,
finely crushed
1 cup butter, softened
1 (15 ounce) container
ricotta cheese

2 teaspoons vanilla
2 large eggs
4 cups flour
2 tablespoons baking
powder
1 teaspoon salt

1½ cups powdered sugar
3 tablespoons milk
4 large peppermint
candy canes,
finely crushed

Cream together sugar, candy canes, and butter, until light and fluffy. Beat in ricotta, vanilla, and eggs until well combined. Combine flour, baking powder, and salt. Mix well. Slowly add flour mixture, a little at a time, until well mixed. Drop dough by tablespoonfuls, about 2 inches apart, onto ungreased cookie sheet. Bake at 350 degrees about 15 minutes, until cookies are very lightly golden. Cool. Mix powdered sugar and milk until smooth. Spread on cookies and immediately sprinkle with crushed candy canes.

Yield: 6 dozen cookies.

16

Chocolate Peppermint Mounds

6 ounces semisweet or dark chocolate chips	10 large peppermint candy canes, crushed	1 cup salted peanuts, chopped
6 ounces butterscotch chips	1 cup shoestring potato sticks, chopped	

In microwave-safe bowl, melt chips, stirring frequently until smooth. Stir in candy canes, potato sticks, and peanuts. Drop by teaspoonfuls onto waxed paper–lined cookie sheets. Refrigerate for 15 minutes or until set.

Yield: 3 dozen cookies.

Candy Cane Cream Cheese Cookies

1 (3 ounce) package
  cream cheese,
  softened
1 cup butter, softened
1 cup sugar

12 large peppermint
  candy canes,
  finely crushed
1 egg yolk
1 tablespoon milk

⅛ teaspoon almond
  extract
2½ cups sifted cake flour
1 cup sliced almonds,
  toasted

Mix together cream cheese, butter, sugar, and crushed candy canes until fluffy. Blend in egg yolk, milk, and almond extract. Gradually stir in flour. Stir in almonds. Divide dough in half and place each half on large sheet of waxed paper. Roll into 1½-inch roll. Chill until very firm. Cut rolls into ¼-inch slices and place on ungreased cookie sheets. Bake at 325 degrees for 10 to 15 minutes or until edges are golden.

Yield: 4 dozen cookies.

Chocolate Mint Bars

1 cup flour
1 cup sugar
½ cup butter, softened

4 eggs
1½ cups chocolate syrup

10 large peppermint
candy canes,
finely crushed

MINT CREAM:
2 cups powdered sugar
2 candy canes, crushed
½ cup butter, softened

1 tablespoon water
½ teaspoon peppermint
extract

CHOCOLATE GLAZE:
6 tablespoons butter
1 cup chocolate chips

Combine first six ingredients in large bowl and beat until smooth. Pour batter into greased 9 x 13-inch baking pan. Bake at 350 degrees for 25 to 30 minutes. Cool completely. Mint cream: Combine sugar, crushed candy canes, softened butter, water, and peppermint extract. Beat until smooth. Spread mint cream on cake. Cover and refrigerate. Chocolate glaze: Melt butter and chips over low heat. Stir until smooth. Cool. Pour over chilled dessert. Cover and refrigerate 1 hour.

Yield: 12 bars.

Peppermint Choco Puffs

¾ cup butter
¼ cup sugar
1 egg yolk
1 teaspoon vanilla

2 cups flour
10 large peppermint
candy canes, finely
crushed

1 egg white
½ cup sugar
Semisweet chocolate
chunks

Cream butter and sugar until fluffy. Stir in egg yolk and vanilla. Add flour a little at a time. Stir in candy canes. Roll dough into 1-inch-thick balls. Beat egg white slightly with fork. Roll each ball in egg white and sugar. Place a chocolate piece in center of each ball. Bake in ungreased pan at 350 degrees for 15 minutes.

Yield: 4 dozen cookies.

Peppermint Cream Fudge Cookies

1 cup sugar	1 egg	2 ounces cream cheese
½ cup unsalted butter, softened	1 cup flour (measure before sifting)	8 large peppermint candy canes, finely crushed
1 teaspoon vanilla	½ teaspoon baking powder	
2 ounces unsweetened chocolate, melted	½ teaspoon salt	

Cream together sugar and butter. Stir in vanilla, chocolate, and egg. Sift flour into chocolate mixture. Add baking powder and salt. Roll into 1½-inch balls and place on ungreased cookie sheet, 2 inches apart. Press a hole in center of each ball. Place cookie sheet in refrigerator for 15 minutes. Stir together cream cheese and crushed candy canes. Remove cookies from refrigerator and fill each hole with peppermint mixture. Bake at 350 degrees for 11 to 12 minutes. Cool.

Yield: 20 cookies.

Sugary Peppermint Paws

¾ cup sugar
10 large peppermint
   candy canes,
   finely crushed

2 sticks butter, softened
2½ cups flour
¼ cup ground pecans
   or almonds

½ cup powdered sugar
3 large peppermint
   candy canes,
   finely crushed

Cream together sugar, crushed candy canes, and butter. Stir in flour and pecans and mix well. Wrap dough in plastic wrap and chill for at least 1 hour. Using buttered madeleine pans (pan with shell-shaped molded indentions), press 2 tablespoons of dough into each shape. Bake at 350 degrees for 15 to 20 minutes or until lightly browned. Immediately remove from pans and roll in mixture of powdered sugar and crushed candy canes. Cool.

Yield: 4 dozen cookies.

Bethlehem Cookies

¾ cup sugar
¾ cup shortening
1 egg
2¼ cups flour

¼ teaspoon salt
1 teaspoon baking
soda

12 large peppermint
candy canes, finely
crushed and divided
¼ cup sugar

Cream sugar, shortening, and egg together. Sift dry ingredients together and add to creamed mixture. Add crushed candy canes to batter, reserving 4 tablespoons. Roll into 1-inch balls. Roll balls in mixture of sugar and remaining crushed candy canes. Bake at 375 degrees for 10 to 12 minutes, until lightly browned.

Yield: 3 dozen cookies.

Minty Eggnog Cookies

2¼ cups flour
1 teaspoon baking
  powder
1 teaspoon allspice
¾ cup salted butter,
  softened

1¼ cups sugar
8 large peppermint
  candy canes,
  finely crushed,
  reserve 4 tablespoons
½ teaspoon vanilla

½ teaspoon peppermint
  extract
2 large egg yolks
½ cup eggnog
Ground nutmeg

Combine flour, baking powder, and allspice, set aside. Cream butter with sugar and crushed candy canes. Add vanilla, peppermint extract, egg yolks, and eggnog. Beat on medium until smooth. Add flour mixture and beat on low just until combined. Drop by teaspoonfuls, 1 inch apart, onto ungreased cookie sheets. Sprinkle with nutmeg and reserved crushed candy canes. Bake at 350 degrees for 20 to 22 minutes or until bottoms are light brown.

Yield: 3 dozen cookies.

Peppermint Cream Brownies

1 (19 ounce) package
brownie mix
8 large peppermint
candy canes,
finely crushed

2 cups powdered sugar
2 tablespoons milk
½ teaspoon peppermint
extract
¼ cup butter

3 (1 ounce) squares
semisweet chocolate
3 tablespoons butter

Mix brownies according to package directions. Stir in crushed candy canes. Pour into 9 x 13-inch pan and bake according to package directions. Cool. Blend sugar, milk, peppermint extract, and butter until smooth and spread over brownies. Melt chocolate and 3 tablespoons butter and spread over peppermint icing.

Yield: 2 dozen brownies.

Chocolate Mint Cookies

¾ cup butter, softened	1 teaspoon vanilla	¼ to ½ teaspoon salt
½ cup sugar	1 egg	8 large peppermint
½ cup brown sugar, packed	1¾ cups flour	candy canes, finely crushed
¼ teaspoon peppermint extract	¼ cup unsweetened cocoa powder	1½ cups of chocolate chips
	1 teaspoon baking soda	

Cream butter and sugars. Add peppermint extract, vanilla, and egg. In separate bowl, mix together flour, cocoa powder, baking soda, salt, and crushed candy canes. Mix flour mixture into creamed mixture. Add chocolate chips. Form dough into tablespoon-sized balls, place on lightly greased cookie sheets, and bake at 350 degrees for 10 minutes. Cool.

Yield: 2 dozen cookies.

Peppermint Wafers

| 1 (10 ounce) bag chocolate cream mints | 8 large peppermint candy canes, finely crushed and divided | 50 vanilla wafers |

Combine chocolate cream mints and half of crushed candy canes in microwave-safe bowl. Cook on high in microwave for several minutes, stirring every 30 seconds until melted. Use thin-tined fork to dip wafers into melted chocolate. Tap fork on edge of bowl to remove excess chocolate before placing wafers onto cold, waxed paper-covered cookie sheet. Sprinkle cookies with remaining crushed candy cane, if desired. Refrigerate until set.

Yield: 50 wafers.

Chocolate Peppermint Cookies

1 (18.25 ounce) package devil's food cake mix
½ cup shortening
1 egg

½ cup milk
½ teaspoon peppermint extract

8 large candy canes, finely crushed and divided

Beat together shortening, egg, milk, peppermint extract, and crushed candy canes (reserving 3 tablespoons) until smooth and creamy. Stir in cake mix. Roll teaspoonfuls of dough into balls and place them 1 inch apart onto greased cookie sheets. Bake at 350 degrees for 8 to 10 minutes. When they start to crack, they are done. Sprinkle with remaining crushed candy canes.

Yield: 2 dozen cookies.

Peppermint Cereal Squares

3 tablespoons butter or margarine

40 large marshmallows
6 cups crisp rice cereal

8 large peppermint candy canes, finely crushed

Over low heat, stir butter and marshmallows until melted and smooth.
Remove from heat. Stir in cereal and crushed candy canes.
Mix well. Press mixture into greased 9 x 13-inch pan.
Cool and cut into squares.

Yield: 12 squares.

Peppermint Stick Cookies

1 cup butter flavored shortening
1 cup powdered sugar, sifted
1 egg
1 teaspoon almond extract
1 teaspoon vanilla
2½ cups flour
1 teaspoon salt
12 large peppermint candy canes, finely crushed and divided
½ teaspoon red food coloring
½ cup sugar

Mix together shortening, powdered sugar, egg, and flavorings. Mix flour, salt, and crushed candy canes (reserving 3 tablespoons). Stir into creamed mixture. Divide dough in half. Blend food coloring into one half. Roll 4-inch strip using 1 teaspoon dough from each color. For smooth, even strips, roll them back and forth on lightly floured board. Place strips side by side, press together lightly and twist like rope. Place on ungreased baking sheet. Bake at 375 degrees for about 9 minutes, until lightly browned. While still warm, sprinkle with mixture of crushed candy canes and sugar.

Yield: 30 cookies.

Candy Cane Meringue Cookies

2 egg whites, room
temperature
⅛ teaspoon salt
⅛ teaspoon cream of
tartar

12 large peppermint
candy canes, finely
crushed
¾ cup sugar
½ teaspoon vanilla

1 cup semisweet
chocolate chips
1 cup walnuts, chopped

Beat egg whites until foamy. Add salt and cream of tartar. Continue beating until soft peaks form. Add crushed candy canes and sugar gradually while continuing to beat to stiff peaks. Stir in vanilla and fold in chocolate chips and walnuts. Drop by heaping teaspoonfuls onto parchment paper–lined cookie sheets. Bake at 250 degrees for 40 minutes. Cool.

Yield: 5 dozen cookies.

Peppermint Snowballs

1 cup butter
½ cup powdered sugar
1 teaspoon vanilla
2¼ cups flour

10 large peppermint
candy canes, finely
crushed and divided
1 cup pecans, chopped

¼ teaspoon salt
½ cup powdered sugar

Cream butter with ½ cup powdered sugar and vanilla. Mix in flour, candy canes (reserving 3 tablespoons), nuts, and salt. Roll about 1 tablespoon of dough into balls. Bake at 350 degrees for 15 minutes on ungreased cookie sheet. Do not allow these cookies to get too brown. Combine remaining powdered sugar and crushed candy canes. While cookies are still hot roll them in sugar mixture. Cool. Roll them in sugar mixture again.

Yield: 5 dozen cookies.

Christmas Eve Cookies

1 cup shortening	12 large peppermint	2¾ cups flour
½ cup sugar	candy canes, finely	1 teaspoon salt
½ cup brown sugar,	crushed and divided	½ teaspoon baking soda
packed	2 eggs	10 ounces dark
	1½ teaspoons vanilla	chocolate chips

Cream together shortening, sugars, and crushed candy canes (reserving 3 tablespoons). Add eggs, one at a time, beating well after each. Beat in vanilla. Combine flour, salt, and baking soda and gradually add to creamed mixture. Shape into 15-inch roll and wrap in plastic wrap. Refrigerate 4 hours. Cut into ⅛-inch slices. Place 2 inches apart on ungreased cookie sheets. Bake at 375 degrees for 6 to 8 minutes or until edges begin to brown. Cool. Melt chocolate chips in microwave, stirring every 30 seconds. Dip half of cookie into melted chocolate and sprinkle with candy canes.

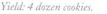

Yield: 4 dozen cookies.

Santa's Favorite Brownies

¾ cup oil
2 cups sugar
2 teaspoons vanilla
4 eggs
1⅓ cups flour

1 cup baking cocoa
1 teaspoon baking powder
1 teaspoon salt

12 large peppermint candy canes, finely crushed and divided
1 cup semisweet chocolate chips
1 tablespoon shortening

Cream together oil and sugar. Stir in vanilla. Add eggs, one at a time, beating well after each addition. Combine flour, cocoa, baking powder, salt, and crushed candy canes (reserving 3 tablespoons). Gradually add to creamed mixture. Spread into 9 x 13-inch pan lined with foil that has been greased. Bake at 350 degrees for 35 to 40 minutes or until a toothpick inserted near center comes out clean. Cool.
Melt chocolate chips and shortening in microwave. Stir until smooth. Spread over brownies and sprinkle with reserved candy.

Yield: 24 brownies.

Royal Candy Cane Cookies

1 cup butter,
  softened
1 cup powdered sugar
1 egg

½ teaspoon peppermint
  extract
½ teaspoon vanilla
2½ cups flour
¼ teaspoon salt

10 large peppermint
  candy canes, finely
  crushed
¼ cup granulated sugar

Cream butter and powdered sugar until light and fluffy. Add egg, peppermint, and vanilla and beat until well blended. Combine flour and salt and gradually add to batter. Mix well. Cover tightly with plastic wrap and chill for 1 hour. Coat baking sheet with nonstick cooking spray. Combine crushed candy canes and sugar. Mix well. Shape chilled dough into 1-inch balls then roll each ball in candy cane mixture. Bake at 350 degrees for 10 to 12 minutes. Cool.

Yield: 36 cookies.

Christmas Yule Bars

1 cup butter	5 drops red food	10 large peppermint
1 cup sugar	coloring	candy canes, finely
1 egg	2 cups flour	crushed and divided
¼ teaspoon peppermint	¼ teaspoon salt	1 cup semisweet
extract		chocolate chips

Cream together butter and sugar. Beat in egg, peppermint extract, and food coloring. Add flour and salt until well blended. Stir in ½ of crushed candy canes. Spread evenly into greased 9 x 13-inch pan. Bake at 350 degrees for 25 minutes or until firm. Cool. Melt chocolate chips in microwave and spread evenly over bars. Sprinkle with remaining candy canes.

Yield: 2 dozen bars.

Snowdrift Peppermint Brownies

1 (19 ounce) package
  brownie mix
½ cup oil
¼ cup water

3 eggs
3 cups peppermint
  ice cream, softened
3 cups whipped topping

6 large candy canes,
  crushed

Prepare brownie mix as directed on package. Bake at 350 degrees for 28 to 30 minutes in 9 x 13-inch foil-lined pan. Cool. Lift brownie from pan with foil. Cut into 10 candy-cane shaped pieces. Place on serving platter. Mound ice cream onto candy cane-shaped brownies and spread evenly. Top with whipped topping, spreading evenly over top and sides. Sprinkle crushed candy canes diagonally on whipped topping. Cover loosely with foil and freeze at least 4 hours.

Yield: 10 brownies.

Minty Chocolate Snowballs

2 cups heavy whipping cream, whipped
1 (16 ounce) package miniature marshmallows
10 large peppermint candy canes, finely crushed
½ cup pecans, chopped
1 (9 ounce) package chocolate wafers, crushed

Combine whipped cream, marshmallows, crushed candy canes, and pecans. Cover and chill for 3 hours. Place wafer crumbs in shallow dish. Stir marshmallow mixture. Scoop out ¼ cupfuls and shape into balls. Roll in crumbs until coated. Chill.

Yield: 20 snowballs.

Chocolate Paws

2⅔ cups flour
2 teaspoons baking
    powder
1 teaspoon salt
1 cup butter

8 large peppermint
    candy canes, finely
    crushed
½ cup chocolate flavored
    syrup
2 eggs

1 teaspoon vanilla
¼ teaspoon peppermint
    extract
¼ cup milk
1 cup peanut halves or
    almond slivers

Sift flour, baking powder, and salt together. Cream butter, sugar, and crushed candy canes until light and fluffy. Stir in syrup and eggs, one at a time, beating well after each. Stir in vanilla and peppermint, then mix in dry ingredients alternately with milk. Chill 1 hour. Drop by heaping teaspoonfuls on greased baking sheet. Insert 4 peanut halves about halfway into the fattest part to resemble claws. Bake at 375 degrees for 10 to 12 minutes.

Yield: 3 dozen paws.

Stained Glass Sugar Cookies

1 cup butter
1 cup shortening
1 cup powdered sugar
1 cup sugar
2 eggs
1 teaspoon vanilla

4½ cups flour
1 teaspoon baking soda
½ teaspoon salt
1 teaspoon cream of tartar

12 large peppermint candy canes, finely crushed
2-inch and 1-inch heart-shaped cookie cutters

Cream together butter, shortening, and sugars. Stir in eggs and vanilla. Add dry ingredients (except crushed candy canes) and mix well. Dough will be greasy. Roll out dough on floured surface and cut into 2-inch, heart-shaped cookies. Then cut out 1-inch heart shape in middle of larger cookies. Put cookies on foil-lined cookie sheet. Inside of cut-out heart, sprinkle crushed candy canes. Spread crumbs to inside edges of cookie. Bake at 350 degrees for 10 to 12 minutes.

Yield: 96 cookies.

Magic Christmas Brownies

4 ounces dark chocolate	½ teaspoon peppermint	8 large peppermint
½ cup unsalted butter	extract	candy canes, finely
2 eggs	1 cup flour	crushed and divided
¼ cup granulated sugar	¼ teaspoon salt	½ cup mini chocolate
1 teaspoon vanilla		chips

Over medium heat, melt chocolate with butter, stirring often. Set aside.
Beat eggs and sugar until light and fluffy and stir in cooled chocolate
mixture, vanilla, and peppermint extract. Beat in flour and salt. Add crushed
candy canes, reserving 3 tablespoons, and chocolate chips. Pour into
8-inch square baking dish with greased and floured foil-lined bottom.
Sprinkle with remaining candy canes.
Bake at 350 degrees for 25 to 30 minutes.
Cool. Serve with vanilla ice cream.

Yield: 8 brownies.

Holiday Sandwich Cookies

36 chocolate wafer cookies

¾ cup unsalted butter, softened

1 cup plus 2 tablespoons powdered sugar

8 large peppermint candy canes, finely crushed

½ teaspoon peppermint extract

2 drops (or more) red food coloring

4 large peppermint candy canes, finely crushed

Cream together butter, sugar, and 8 crushed candy canes. Add peppermint extract and 2 drops food coloring. Beat until light pink and well blended, adding 1 to 2 more drops of food coloring. Lay out half of wafer cookies. Spread 2 generous teaspoons of filling evenly over flat side of each to edges. Top with remaining cookies, flat side down. Place remaining crushed candy canes on plate. Roll edges of cookie sandwiches firmly in crushed candy canes.

Yield: 18 cookies.

Festive Peppermint Balls

1 cup butter
12 large peppermint
   candy canes, finely
   crushed and divided

1½ cups powdered sugar
1 teaspoon vanilla
2⅓ cups flour

2 tablespoons cream
   cheese
1 teaspoon milk

Cream butter with half of crushed candy canes, and ½ cup powdered sugar. Mix in vanilla, then flour. Roll dough into balls and make a deep well in center of each ball. Filling: Combine cream cheese and milk. Add ½ cup powdered sugar slowly. Stir in 4 tablespoons of crushed candy canes. Fill with ¼ teaspoon of filling. To cover hole, shape small pieces of dough into flat rounds and press gently to seal. Bake at 350 degrees on ungreased cookie sheet for 12 minutes. Combine remaining powdered sugar and crushed candy canes and roll warm cookies in the mixture.

Yield: 3 dozen cookies.

Peppermint Snowdrops

1 cup butter, softened
1 cup sugar
6 large peppermint candy canes, finely crushed
½ teaspoon almond extract
½ teaspoon peppermint extract
1 egg, slightly beaten
2 cups flour
½ cup pecans, finely chopped
6 large peppermint candy canes, finely crushed
½ cup sugar

Cream together butter, sugar, and 6 crushed candy canes. Add almond and peppermint extracts. Add egg and beat until fluffy. Beat in flour and nuts until mixture is lightly moistened. Chill for 1 hour. Shape dough into 1-inch balls. Place 2 inches apart on greased cookie sheet. Dip flat-bottomed glass into sugar and press balls to a ¼-inch thickness. Sprinkle with mixture of remaining crushed candy canes and sugar. Bake at 350 degrees for 10 to 12 minutes.

Yield: 3 dozen cookies.

Candy Cane Macaroons

⅓ cup butter, softened
1 (3 ounce) package
   cream cheese, softened
¾ cup sugar
10 large peppermint
   candy canes, finely
   crushed

1 egg yolk
2 teaspoons strong
   coffee
2 teaspoons almond
   extract
1¼ cups flour

2 teaspoons baking
   powder
¼ teaspoon salt
1 (14 ounce) package
   flaked coconut, divided

Cream together butter, cream cheese, sugar, and candy canes. Add egg yolk, coffee, and almond extract. Mix well. Combine flour, baking powder, and salt in separate bowl. Slowly add flour mixture to creamed mixture. Stir in 3 cups of coconut. Chill dough for 1 hour. Roll dough into 1-inch balls. Roll each in coconut. Place on ungreased baking sheet and flatten with fork. Bake at 350 degrees for 12 to 15 minutes. Cool.

Yield: 3 dozen cookies.

Minty Mocha Cookies

2 sticks butter, softened
½ cup sugar
10 large peppermint
candy canes, finely
crushed
1½ teaspoons vanilla

⅛ teaspoon peppermint
extract
2 cups sifted flour
½ teaspoon salt
1 tablespoon powdered
instant coffee
¼ cup cocoa

1 cup nuts, finely
chopped
½ cup maraschino
cherries, chopped
6 large peppermint
candy canes, finely
crushed

Cream together butter, sugar, and 10 crushed candy canes until light and fluffy. Stir in vanilla and peppermint. In separate bowl, combine flour, salt, instant coffee, and cocoa. Mix well before blending into creamed mixture, a little at a time. Stir in nuts and cherries. Cover and chill until dough can be easily handled. Form dough into 1-inch balls. Place on greased cookie sheet. Bake at 325 degrees for 2 minutes or until lightly browned. Dust warm cookies with remaining crushed candy canes.

Yield: 60 cookies.

No-Bake Cherry Mint Crisps

¼ cup butter, softened
1 cup peanut butter
1 cup powdered sugar
8 large peppermint
   candy canes, finely
   crushed

1⅓ cups crisp rice cereal
½ cup maraschino
   cherries, drained,
   dried, and chopped

¼ cup plus 2 tablespoons
   mini semisweet
   chocolate chips
¼ cup chopped pecans
1 to 2 cups flaked
   coconut

Cream together butter, peanut butter, sugar, and crushed candy canes.

Stir in cereal, cherries, chocolate chips, and pecans. Mix well.

Shape teaspoonfuls of dough into 1-inch balls. Roll in coconut.

Place on cookie sheets and refrigerate 1 hour.

Store in refrigerator.

Yield: 3 dozen cookies.

Fudgy Minty No-Bake Treats

2 cups sugar
½ cup butter
½ cup milk
⅓ cup baking cocoa

10 large peppermint
  candy canes, finely
  crushed
⅔ cup crunchy peanut
  butter

3 cups quick-cooking
  rolled oats
½ cup peanuts, chopped
2 teaspoons vanilla

Combine sugar, butter, milk, cocoa, and crushed candy canes in medium saucepan. Cook over medium heat, stirring constantly, until mixture comes to a rolling boil. Remove from heat and cool 1 minute. Add peanut butter, oats, peanuts, and vanilla. Mix well. Immediately drop by heaping teaspoonfuls onto waxed paper- or foil-covered cookie sheet. Cool.

Yield: 3 dozen treats.

Mocha Peppermint Crinkles

1⅓ cups brown sugar,
  packed
12 large peppermint
  candy canes, finely
  crushed
½ cup oil
¼ cup sour cream

1 egg
1 teaspoon vanilla
1¾ cups flour
¾ cup unsweetened
  cocoa powder
2 teaspoons instant
  espresso

1 teaspoon baking soda
¼ teaspoon salt
⅛ teaspoon black pepper
½ cup powdered sugar
4 large peppermint
  candy canes, finely
  crushed

Beat together sugar, crushed candy canes, and oil. Add sour cream, egg, and vanilla. Mix well and set aside. Combine flour, cocoa, espresso, baking soda, salt, and pepper. Add flour mixture to sugar mixture. Mix well. Refrigerate dough 3 to 4 hours. Mix powdered sugar and crushed candy canes in small bowl. Roll dough into 1-inch balls. Roll balls in sugar mixture. Bake at 375 degrees on ungreased cookie sheets for 10 to 12 minutes.

Yield: 6 dozen cookies.

Double Chocolate Mint Oat Cookies

2 cups semisweet
   chocolate pieces,
   divided
½ cup butter, softened
½ cup sugar

10 large peppermint
   candy canes, finely
   crushed
1 egg
¼ teaspoon vanilla

¾ cup flour
¾ cup rolled oats
1 teaspoon baking
   powder
¼ teaspoon baking soda

Melt 1 cup chocolate pieces in small saucepan and set aside. Cream together butter, sugar, and crushed candy canes until fluffy. Add melted chocolate, egg, and vanilla. Combine flour, oats, baking powder, and baking soda. Add a little at a time to chocolate mixture until well incorporated. Stir in remaining chocolate pieces. Drop by rounded teaspoonfuls onto ungreased cookie sheets. Bake at 375 degrees for 8 to 10 minutes. Cool.

Yield: 3 dozen cookies.

Fiesta Chocolate Mint Macaroons

8 ounces semisweet
   baking chocolate
1¾ cups plus ⅓ cup
   whole almonds,
   divided

¾ cup sugar
8 large peppermint
   candy canes, coarsely
   chopped
1 teaspoon ground
   cinnamon

1 teaspoon vanilla
2 egg whites
3 large peppermint
   candy canes, finely
   crushed

Coarsely chop 5 ounces of chocolate in food processor. Add 1¾ cups almonds, sugar, and chopped candy canes. Pulse mixture until finely ground. Add cinnamon, vanilla, and egg whites. Pulse until mixture forms moist dough. Form dough into 1-inch balls. Roll balls in finely crushed candy canes before placing on greased cookie sheets 2 inches apart. Press a whole almond on top of each cookie. Bake at 400 degrees for 8 to 10 minutes. Cool. Melt remaining chocolate and drizzle over cookies.

Yield: 3 dozen cookies.

Christmas Carolers Cookies

1 cup butter
1 cup brown sugar
1 egg
2 cups flour, sifted

1 teaspoon baking soda
¼ teaspoon salt
2 cups quick-cooking
  oatmeal

8 large peppermint
  candy canes, coarsely
  chopped

GLAZE:
1½ cups powdered sugar,
  sifted

3 tablespoons milk
1 drop red food coloring

3 tablespoons pepper-
  mint candy canes,
  finely crushed

Cream together butter and sugar until light and fluffy. Blend in egg. Sift
together flour, baking soda, and salt. Add to creamed mixture. Stir in
oatmeal and chopped candy canes. Mix well. Roll into 1-inch balls and
bake on greased cookie sheet at 350 degrees for 8 to 10 minutes. Glaze:
Combine sugar, milk, and food coloring. Mix well. Drizzle on cookies
and sprinkle with crushed candy canes.

Yield: 3 dozen cookies.

Christmas Haystacks

6 ounces chocolate chips
6 ounces butterscotch chips

10 large peppermint candy canes, finely crushed

6 ounces Chow Mein noodles, uncooked

Melt chocolate and butterscotch chips together in double boiler. Blend together thoroughly. Stir in crushed candy canes. Pour noodles into large bowl and add chocolate mixture. Stir until well mixed. Drop by teaspoonfuls onto waxed paper. Refrigerate until firm.

Yield: 3 dozen cookies.

Peppermint Snaps

¼ cup light corn syrup	½ teaspoon vanilla	10 large peppermint
¼ cup molasses	1 cup flour	candy canes, finely
½ cup butter	⅔ cup sugar	crushed

In saucepan, bring syrup and molasses to boil. Remove from heat and add butter and vanilla. Sift together flour, sugar, and crushed candy canes. Stir into molasses mixture. Drop ½ teaspoon of dough, 3 inches apart on cookie sheet. Cookies will spread while baking. Bake at 300 degrees for 10 minutes. Loosen one cookie at a time and roll each over handle of wooden spoon. Slip off carefully. If the cookies get too hard, return to oven for a few minutes to soften.

Yield: 2 dozen cookies.

Cakes and Pies

Fail not to call to mind, in the course of the twenty-fifth of this month,
that the Divinest Heart that ever walked the earth was born on that day;
and then smile and enjoy yourselves for the rest of it;
for mirth is also of Heaven's making.

LEIGH HUNT

Flourless Chocolate Mint Cake

9 ounces semisweet or dark chocolate chips

8 large peppermint candy canes, finely crushed

4 ounces sweet butter

7 egg yolks

7 egg whites

⅓ cup sugar

3 large peppermint candy canes, finely crushed

Grease and flour 9-inch springform pan. Put butter in double boiler before adding chocolate and crushed candy canes. Cook over low heat until chocolate melts. Don't stir until chocolate is melted. Remove from heat and whisk in egg yolks. Whip egg whites, adding sugar slowly as whites start to foam. Whip to medium peaks, do not overwhip. Fold into chocolate mixture. Pour into prepared pan and bake at 275 degrees for 40 to 45 minutes. Remove from oven and run knife around edge. Allow to cool and fall. Dust cake with powdered sugar mixed with finely crushed candy canes. Serve with sweetened whipped cream.

Yield: 10 to 12 slices.

Double Chocolate Mint Muffins

1¼ cups whole wheat flour	½ teaspoon baking soda	¾ cup milk
¼ cup cocoa powder	½ teaspoon salt	2 tablespoons oil
½ cup brown sugar	10 large peppermint candy canes, finely crushed, reserve 3 tablespoons	½ cup semisweet chocolate chips
½ teaspoon baking powder		

ICING:
1 tablespoon cocoa

½ cup powdered sugar
2 tablespoons water

⅛ teaspoon peppermint extract

Mix together flour, cocoa powder, sugar, baking powder, baking soda, salt, and crushed candy canes. Combine milk and oil before adding to dry mixture and mix until dry bits are gone. Do not over mix. Gently stir in chocolate chips. Pour batter into sprayed muffin cups in muffin pan. Bake at 350 degrees for 20 minutes. Cool. Icing: Sift together cocoa and powdered sugar. Heat water in microwave. Add peppermint and whisk together. Spread over muffins and sprinkle with crushed candy canes.

Yield: 8 muffins.

Chocolate Peppermint Dessert

1 (18.25 ounce) package devil's food cake mix
½ teaspoon peppermint extract
10 large peppermint candy canes, finely crushed and divided
1½ cups whipping cream
¼ cup powdered sugar
¼ teaspoon peppermint extract
2 to 3 drops red food coloring

Prepare cake mix as directed on package. Stir in peppermint extract and half of crushed candy canes. Pour into 2 greased and floured round cake pans. Bake as directed. Cool 10 minutes. Remove from pans and cool completely. Beat whipping cream and powdered sugar in chilled bowl until stiff. Add peppermint extract and food coloring the last minute of beating. Stir in remaining crushed candy canes. Stack cakes, frosting between layers and on top. Refrigerate until set, 2 to 3 hours.

Yield: 1 (2 layer) cake.

Three Kings Cake

1 (18.25 ounce) package
   chocolate cake mix
12 large peppermint
   candy canes, finely
   crushed and divided
1 cup whipping cream

⅛ teaspoon peppermint
   extract
1 (16 ounce) container
   prepared white
   chocolate frosting

Prepare cake mix according to directions on package. Add crushed candy canes to batter, reserving 4 tablespoons. Bake at 350 degrees in waxed paper–lined jelly roll pan (cookie sheet with sides). When cooled, cut into 3 pieces for 3 layers. Whip 1 cup whipping cream. When whipped, gently stir in peppermint extract. Put in between layers. Ice heavily with white chocolate frosting, warmed in microwave. Sprinkle remaining crushed candy canes on top.

Yield: 10 to 12 slices.

Frozen Peppermint Cheesecake

1¼ cups chocolate cookie crumbs (about 24 cookies), divided
2 large peppermint candy canes, finely crushed
¼ cup sugar
¼ cup butter, melted
1 (8 ounce) package cream cheese
1 (14 ounce) can sweetened condensed milk
1 to 2 drops of red food coloring
2 cups whipping cream, whipped
10 large peppermint candy canes, finely crushed and divided

Mix together cookie crumbs, 2 crushed candy canes, sugar, and butter. Press into 9-inch pie pan. Combine cream cheese, milk, food coloring, and whipping cream. Pour into pie shell. Sprinkle remaining cookie crumbs mixture and crushed candy canes on top.
Freeze and serve frozen.

Yield: 10 to 12 small slices.

Shepherds Cake

1 (18.25 ounce) package white cake mix
¼ teaspoon peppermint extract

10 large peppermint candy canes, finely crushed and divided
4 drops red food coloring

1 (15 ounce) can white frosting
¼ teaspoon peppermint extract

Mix cake according to package directions for 2-layer cake. Add peppermint extract, crushed candy canes (reserving 3 tablespoons), and food coloring to mixture. Bake as directed. Cool. Mix white frosting with peppermint extract. Frost. Garnish with crushed candy canes.

Yield: 10 to 12 small slices.

Chocolate Christmas Cupcakes

5 (1 ounce) squares semisweet chocolate, divided

1 (18.25 ounce) package chocolate cake mix

1 (3.9 ounce) package chocolate instant pudding

10 small candy canes, finely crushed

4 eggs

1 cup sour cream

½ cup oil

½ cup water

1 (8 ounce) tub whipped topping

6 large peppermint candy canes, finely crushed and divided

Chop 4 chocolate squares. Set aside. On low speed, mix together cake mix, pudding mix, 10 small crushed candy canes, eggs, sour cream, oil, and water until moistened. On medium speed, beat 2 minutes more. Stir in chopped chocolate and 3 tablespoons crushed candy canes. Spoon into paper-lined muffin tins. Bake at 350 degrees for 20 minutes. Cool. Frost cupcakes with whipped topping. Melt remaining chocolate and drizzle over cupcakes. Top with remaining crushed candy canes right before serving.

Yield: 30 cupcakes.

No-Bake Candy Cane Cheesecake Bites

1 pint heavy cream,
  chilled
12 ounces cream cheese,
  softened
¾ cup sugar

10 large peppermint
  candy canes, finely
  crushed and divided
1½ teaspoons vanilla

Whip heavy cream until soft peaks form. Gently transfer whipped cream to separate bowl and set aside. Combine cream cheese, sugar, crushed candy canes, and vanilla. Gently beat cream cheese mixture until fluffy. Fold whipped cream into cream cheese mixture. Spray mini-muffin tin with cooking spray and spoon mixture into cups. Sprinkle each with candy canes, gently pressing them into cheesecake batter. Place in freezer for 6 to 8 hours. When ready to serve, tap muffin tin on counter to loosen.

Yield: 24 bites.

Peppermint Cheesecake

1 cup chocolate wafer
    crumbs
3 tablespoons butter,
    melted
1 envelope unflavored
    gelatin
¼ cup cold water

2 (8 ounce) containers
    cream cheese,
    softened
½ cup sugar
½ cup milk

10 large peppermint
    candy canes, finely
    crushed and divided
1 cup whipping cream,
    whipped
2 (1.05 ounce) milk
    chocolate candy bars,
    finely chopped

Combine crumbs and butter and press onto bottom of 9-inch springform pan. Bake at 350 degrees for 10 minutes. Cool. Soften gelatin in cold water and stir over low heat until dissolved. Combine cream cheese and sugar, mixing with electric mixer until well blended. Gradually add gelatin, milk, and candy canes (reserving 3 tablespoons), until well blended. Chill until slightly thickened. Fold in whipped cream and chocolate. Pour over crust. Chill until firm. Garnish with additional whipped cream and crushed candy canes, if desired.

Yield: 10 to 12 slices.

Candy Cane Cake

1 (18.25-ounce) box white
cake mix
8 large peppermint candy
canes, finely
crushed

1 (15-ounce) can white
frosting
3 large peppermint
candy canes, finely
crushed

Mix cake according to package directions. Stir in 8 crushed candy canes
and pour into bundt cake pan. Bake cake according to package directions.
Cool completely and remove from pan. Frost cake and sprinkle
with remaining crushed candy canes.

Yield: 10 to 12 slices.

Candy Cane Coffee Cake

2 cups flour
1 cup brown sugar, packed
½ cup sugar
10 large peppermint candy canes, coarsely chopped
½ cup butter or margarine, chilled
1 teaspoon baking soda
1 teaspoon salt
1 egg
1 cup buttermilk
1 teaspoon vanilla
3 (1.4 ounce) Heath candy bars, crushed
1 cup pecans, chopped

Combine flour, sugars, and crushed candy canes. Cut in butter until mixture resembles coarse crumbs. Reserve ½ cup for topping. To remaining crumb mixture, add baking soda and salt. Beat egg, buttermilk, and vanilla. Add to crumb mixture and mix well. Pour into greased 11 x 7-inch baking pan. Combine candy bars, pecans, and reserved crumb mixture. Sprinkle over top. Bake at 350 degrees for 40 minutes.

Yield: 8 slices.

Chocolate Hazelnut Cheesecake

⅓ box chocolate graham crackers

3 large peppermint candy canes, finely crushed

¼ cup plus 2 tablespoons butter, melted

1¼ cups milk, chilled

2 tablespoons hazelnut flavor instant coffee powder

8 large peppermint candy canes, finely crushed

2 (4 ounce) packages white chocolate flavor instant pudding

1 (8 ounce) tub whipped topping

2 large peppermint candy canes, coarsely chopped

½ cup dark chocolate chips, chopped

Combine graham crackers, 3 crushed candy canes, and butter. Press into bottom of 9-inch pie pan. In large bowl, whisk together milk, coffee powder, and 8 crushed candy canes. Add pudding mix. Beat with whisk for 1 minute. Whisk in half of whipped topping. Spread in crust. Top with remaining whipped topping. Sprinkle with 2 chopped candy canes and chocolate. Refrigerate for 1 hour.

Yield: 10 to 12 slices.

Candy Cane Cream Pie

1½ cups chocolate wafer crumbs

¼ cup plus 2 tablespoons butter, melted

1 pint peppermint ice cream, softened

4 peppermint candy canes, finely crushed

1 (8 ounce) tub whipped topping

2 peppermint candy canes, coarsely chopped

Combine crumbs and melted butter; press firmly into 9-inch pie pan. Combine ice cream and 4 crushed candy canes. Fold in whipped topping and spoon into crumb crust. Sprinkle with coarsely chopped candy canes; freeze until firm.

Yield: 10 to 12 slices.

Peppermint Candy Pie

24 chocolate cream-filled cookies, crushed
¼ cup butter, melted

1 pint vanilla ice cream, softened
8 large peppermint candy canes, crushed

1 (8 ounce) tub whipped topping
1 tablespoon chocolate sauce

Combine cookie crumbs and butter. Press into bottom and sides of 9-inch pie pan. Combine ice cream and crushed candy canes, then blend in food coloring. Fold in whipped topping. Pour into crust. Drizzle chocolate sauce over pie. Freeze until firm. Remove from freezer 5 minutes before serving.

Yield: 10 to 12 slices.

Easy Frozen Mint Cheesecake

1¼ cups chocolate graham cracker crumbs (about 24 crackers)
¼ cup sugar
¼ cup butter, melted
1 (8 ounce) package cream cheese, softened
1 (14 ounce) can sweetened condensed milk
10 large peppermint candy canes, finely crushed
2 cups whipping cream, whipped

Combine crumbs, sugar, and butter. Press on bottoms and halfway up sides of two 9-inch springform pans or pie pans. In large mixing bowl, beat cream cheese until fluffy. Gradually beat in milk. Stir in crushed candy canes. Fold in whipped cream. Pour into prepared pans and cover. Freeze 6 hours or until firm.

Yield: 20 to 24 slices.

70

Peppermint Punch Bowl Cake

1 (18.25 ounce) box
chocolate cake mix
8 large peppermint
candy canes, finely
crushed

1 large package instant
chocolate pudding
1 (12 ounce) tub
whipped topping
1 cup milk

6 large peppermint
candy canes, coarsely
chopped

Prepare cake according to package instructions. Stir crushed candy canes
into batter before pouring into baking pan. Bake at 350 degrees on cookie
sheet with sides for 20 minutes. Cool and cut into 1-inch cubes. Make
pudding according to package directions. Add 1 extra cup milk.
In punchbowl or trifle dish, layer ⅓ cake cubes, ⅓ pudding,
⅓ whipped topping, and ⅓ of the chopped candy canes.
Repeat 2 more times. Garnish with a whole candy cane.

Yield: 24 servings.

Peppermint Patty Pie

43 peppermint patties
2 (3 ounce) packages
   cream cheese,
   softened

½ cup sugar
6 large peppermint
   candy canes, finely
   crushed and divided

3 (16 ounce) tubs
   whipped topping
2 (9 inch) graham
   cracker pie shells

Chop up 30 peppermint patties in blender or food processor. Mix together cream cheese, chopped peppermint patties, sugar, crushed candy canes (reserving 6 to 8 tablespoons), and 2 whipped topping tubs. Spread mixture evenly in pie shells. Top with remaining whipped topping and sprinkle with remaining crushed candy canes. Garnish each slice with ¼ of a peppermint patty.

Yield: 20 to 24 slices.

Chocolate Mint Muffins

1½ cups whole wheat flour
½ cup unsweetened cocoa

1 tablespoon baking powder
1 cup brown sugar
10 candy canes, finely crushed and divided

2 large eggs
1 cup milk
6 tablespoons canola oil

Combine flour, cocoa, baking powder, sugar, and crushed candy canes (reserving 3 tablespoons). Set aside. Combine eggs, milk, and oil. Pour into dry mixture. Mix until just combined, then bake in well-greased mini muffin cups at 350 degrees for 8 to 11 minutes. While still warm, sprinkle tops with reserved crushed candy canes.

Yield: 2 dozen muffins.

Peppermint Fudge Pie

24 chocolate wafer cookies, crushed
½ cup butter, melted
4 cups miniature marshmallows
½ cup milk
1 cup heavy whipping cream
10 large peppermint candy canes, finely crushed

Combine cookies and butter. Press into 9-inch pie pan. Bake at 350 degrees for 10 minutes. Cool. Put 3 cups marshmallows in double boiler. Add milk, and stir until mixture melts and thickens. Cool in refrigerator 15 minutes. In another bowl, whip cream. Blend in crushed candy canes and remaining marshmallows. Fold whipped cream mixture into melted and cooled marshmallow mixture. Pour into crust, and chill well.

Yield: 10 to 12 slices.

Advent Cheesecake

1⅓ cups chocolate
   cookie crumbs
2 tablespoons sugar
¼ cup butter, melted
1½ cups sour cream
½ cup sugar

3 large eggs
1 tablespoon flour
2 teaspoons vanilla
¼ teaspoon peppermint
   extract
24 ounces cream cheese

2 tablespoons butter
8 large peppermint
   candy canes, finely
   crushed
1 tub whipped topping

Combine cookie crumbs, sugar, and butter. Press into 9-inch springform pan. Blend sour cream, sugar, eggs, flour, vanilla, and peppermint extract until smooth. Add cream cheese and 2 tablespoons butter. Stir in crushed candy canes. Pour into crust and bake at 325 degrees on lowest rack of oven for 50 to 60 minutes. Allow to cool (top may crack) and refrigerate overnight. Immediately before serving, top with whipped topping and sprinkle with crushed candy canes.

Yield: 10 to 12 slices.

Chocolate Mint Cupcakes

¾ cup apple sauce
3 large eggs
1 cup apple juice
¼ teaspoon peppermint
  extract
¼ cup of wheat germ

8 large peppermint
  candy canes, finely
  crushed
1 (18 ounce) box of
  chocolate cake mix

1 (15 ounce) can
  chocolate frosting
6 large peppermint
  candy canes, finely
  crushed

Spray muffin tin (lined with muffin cups). Combine apple sauce, eggs, apple juice, peppermint extract, wheat germ, crushed candy canes, and cake mix. Blend at low speed for 30 seconds, then increase speed to medium for another 2 minutes. Pour batter into muffin cups. Bake at 350 degrees for 15 minutes. Combine frosting and crushed candy canes. Mix thoroughly. Ice cupcakes and serve.

Yield: 12 cupcakes.

Desserts and Candies

There has been only one Christmas—the rest are anniversaries.

W. J. CAMERON

Candy Kisses

2 egg whites
¼ teaspoon salt
⅛ teaspoon cream of
tartar

½ cup sugar
6 peppermint candy
canes, finely crushed

Beat egg whites till foamy. Add salt and cream of tartar. Beat to soft peaks. Beat in sugar, 1 tablespoon at a time, until stiff and glossy. Pour into plastic bag. Snip off one corner to make a small hole. Squeeze out on ungreased foil- or parchment-lined cookie sheets. Bake at 225 degrees for 1½ to 2 hours, until very dry but not browned.

Yields 3 dozen kisses.

Chocolate Peppermint Truffles

8 ounces semisweet chocolate, chopped
½ cup heavy cream

3 tablespoons unsalted butter, softened and cut up

10 large peppermint candy canes, finely crushed and divided
3 tablespoons unsweetened cocoa

Process chocolate and candy canes in food processor until finely ground (reserving 3 tablespoons). In saucepan, heat heavy cream over medium heat to boiling. Add cream to chocolate mixture in food processor and blend until smooth. Add butter and blend well. Line 9 x 5-inch pan with plastic wrap. Pour chocolate mixture into pan; spread evenly. Refrigerate 3 hours, until firm enough to handle. Remove chocolate mixture from pan by lifting edges of plastic wrap and inverting block onto cutting board. Cut chocolate block into 32 pieces. Mix reserved crushed candy canes with unsweetened cocoa. Quickly roll each chocolate piece into a ball, then roll balls in cocoa mixture and refrigerate.

Yield: 32 truffles.

Chocolate Mint Chips

24 ounces white candy
coating
14 ounces thick, ripple
potato chips
24 ounces dark choco-
late candy coating

12 large peppermint
candy canes, finely
crushed and divided

Stirring occasionally, melt white coating in microwave until smooth.
Dip chips halfway in coating and shake off excess. Place on chilled, waxed
paper-lined baking sheets and place in refrigerator for 5 minutes. Stirring
occasionally, melt dark chocolate coating in microwave until melted and
smooth. Stir in crushed candy canes. Dip other half of chips in coating
and shake off excess. Place on chilled, waxed paper-lined baking sheets
to set. Immediately sprinkle with remaining crushed candy canes and
place in refrigerator for 5 minutes.

Yield: 2 pounds.

Peppermint Almond Crunch

¾ cup flaked coconut
1½ cups sugar
3 tablespoons water
1 tablespoon light corn
   syrup

½ cup butter
¾ cup sliced almonds
6 large peppermint
   candy canes, coarsely
   chopped

½ cup semisweet
   chocolate chips
4 large peppermint
   candy canes, finely
   crushed

Line 9 x 13-inch pan with foil and spray with cooking spray. Spread coconut evenly into prepared pan. Set aside. In large saucepan, combine sugar, water, and corn syrup. Bring to a boil over medium heat, stirring occasionally. Add butter and stir until butter is melted. Continue cooking, without stirring, until candy thermometer reads 300 degrees. Remove from heat. Stir in almonds and chopped candy canes. Pour over coconut. Cool. Melt chocolate chips in the microwave, stirring constantly. Remove; stir until smooth. Stir in crushed candy canes. Drizzle over candy. Cool until firm. Remove from foil and break into pieces.

Yield: 36 pieces.

Peppermint Toffee

4 ounces saltine crackers	4 large peppermint candy canes, finely crushed	¾ cup pecans, chopped
1 cup butter		3 large peppermint candy canes, finely crushed
1 cup dark brown sugar	2 cups semisweet chocolate chips	

Line cookie sheet with saltine crackers in a single layer. In saucepan combine butter, sugar, and 4 crushed candy canes. Boil for 3 minutes. Immediately spread over crackers. Bake at 400 degrees for 5 to 6 minutes. Remove from oven and sprinkle chocolate chips over top. Let sit for 5 minutes. Spread melted chocolate and top with chopped nuts and remaining crushed candy canes. Cool completely and break into pieces.

Yield: 36 pieces.

Crunchy Peppermint Cups

12 ounces semisweet chocolate chips

12 ounces butterscotch chips

12 ounces peanut butter chips

10 large peppermint candy canes, finely chopped

1 cup cornflakes, chopped

½ cup peanuts, chopped

In large saucepan, melt chips over low heat or in microwave, stirring constantly. When melted, remove from heat and add chopped candy canes, cornflakes, and peanuts. Drop by teaspoonfuls into miniature foil cups placed on cookie sheet. Refrigerate until firm.

Yield: 5 dozen cups.

Peppermint Chocolate Roll

6 eggs
½ cup plus 2 tablespoons sugar
10 large peppermint candy canes, finely crushed

6 tablespoons unsweetened cocoa
1 teaspoon vanilla
⅛ teaspoon peppermint extract

2 cups whipping cream, whipped
⅓ teaspoon peppermint extract

Grease jelly roll pan. Line with greased waxed paper. Separate egg yolks from whites and beat yolks until thick and creamy. Add sugar and crushed candy canes gradually, continue beating. Stir in cocoa, vanilla, and peppermint extract. Beat egg whites until stiff peaks form. Gently fold into cocoa mixture. Pour into greased jelly roll pan lined with greased waxed paper. Bake at 350 degrees for 25 minutes. While cake bakes, sprinkle a piece of foil with powdered sugar. Beat whipping cream, fold in extract. Remove cake from oven, invert onto foil and remove paper. Roll cake lengthwise. When cooled, unroll and spread with whipped cream before rerolling.

Yield: 10 slices.

Minty Apple Turnovers

2 whole green apples
2 (8 ounce) tubes
  crescent rolls
2 sticks butter

1½ cups sugar
1 teaspoon vanilla
1 (12 ounce) can lemon-
  lime soda

2 teaspoons cinnamon
4 large peppermint
  candy canes, finely
  crushed

Peel and core apples. Cut each apple into 8 slices. Roll each apple slice in a crescent roll. Place in 9 x 13-inch buttered pan. Melt butter, then add sugar and barely stir. Add vanilla and stir. Pour entire mixture over apples. Pour can of lemon-lime beverage around edges of pan. Mix cinnamon and crushed candy canes and sprinkle on top. Bake at 350 degrees for 40 minutes. Serve with ice cream, drizzling sauce from pan over top.

Yield: 16 slices.

Chocolate Candy Cane Marshmallows

1 (16 ounce) package jumbo marshmallows
1 (10 ounce) bag white chocolate chips

1 (10 ounce) bag dark chocolate chips

12 large peppermint candy canes, finely crushed

Place toothpick in end of marshmallow. Melt white chocolate chips. Dip half of marshmallows into white chocolate and then into crushed peppermint candy canes. Place on chilled cookie sheet and place in refrigerator. Melt dark chocolate chips and repeat dipping process with remaining marshmallows.

Yield: 30 marshmallows.

Candy Cane Cake Balls

1 (18.25 ounce) box
white cake mix
½ teaspoon peppermint
extract

1 (16 ounce) container
vanilla frosting,
softened in microwave
2 (10 ounce) bags milk
chocolate chips

12 large peppermint
candy canes,
finely crushed
and divided

Prepare cake mix according to box instructions. Stir in ½ teaspoon peppermint extract and half of crushed peppermint candy canes before pouring into pans. Bake as directed. After cake is cooked, crumble into large bowl while still warm. Add frosting to crumbled cake. Roll mixture into quarter-sized balls and place on waxed paper-covered cookie sheet. Place in freezer for 1 hour. Heat chocolate in microwave, stirring occasionally, until melted and smooth. Using thin-tined fork dip cake balls into melted chocolate, tapping fork on side of bowl to remove excess chocolate. Return dipped balls to chilled cookie sheet and sprinkle with remaining crushed candy canes.

Yield: 40 cake balls.

Cream Cheese Peppermint Candies

1 (3 ounce) package
  cream cheese,
  softened

10 large peppermint
  candy canes, finely
  crushed and divided

¼ teaspoon peppermint
  extract
3 cups powdered sugar

In small mixing bowl, beat cream cheese with crushed candy canes (reserving 4 tablespoons) and peppermint extract. Add half the sugar and beat until smooth. Knead in remaining sugar until fully incorporated. Shape dough into ½-inch balls, place on baking sheets, flatten with fork and sprinkle with reserved crushed candy canes. Let sit for 1 hour.

Yield: 72 candies.

Candy Cane Biscotti

48 biscotti biscuits
14 ounces melted white
chocolate

8 large peppermint candy
canes, finely crushed

Dip half of each biscotti biscuit into melted chocolate.
Shake off excess. Immediately roll in crushed candy canes
and set on chilled baking sheet lined with waxed paper.
Let set until chocolate has set.

Yield: 4 dozen biscotti.

Holiday Peppermint Peanut Brittle

2¾ cups sugar
6 large peppermint
candy canes, finely
crushed

½ stick unsalted butter
⅔ cup water
1½ cups lightly salted
peanuts

6 large peppermint
candy canes, coarsely
chopped

In large saucepan over medium heat, cook sugar, crushed candy canes, butter, and water. Stir constantly until mixture becomes a golden-brown syrup, about 25 minutes. Remove from heat and stir in peanuts and chopped candy canes. Pour mixture into greased and foil-lined 9 x 13-inch pan. Cool before breaking into pieces.

Yield: 36 pieces.

Peppermint Twists

| 12 frozen heat and serve dinner rolls, thawed but still cold | 1 cup powdered sugar 2 to 3 tablespoons milk | 3 large peppermint candy canes, finely crushed |

Cut each roll in half. Roll each half into an 8-inch rope. Twist two ropes together and pinch ends together. Place on large greased baking sheet. Cover with greased plastic wrap and let rise 30 minutes. Remove wrap and bake at 350 degrees for 10 to15 minutes. Combine powdered sugar and milk and brush over warm twists. Sprinkle with crushed peppermint candy.

Yield: 12 twists.

Candy Cane Puffs

2½ cups flour
¼ teaspoon salt
½ cup unsalted butter, softened
1 cup powdered sugar
1 egg

½ teaspoon peppermint extract
½ teaspoon vanilla

8 (1 ounce) squares white chocolate, melted
6 large peppermint candy canes, finely crushed

Stir together flour and salt in medium-sized bowl. Beat butter and sugar in large bowl until smooth and creamy. Beat in egg. Mix in peppermint extract and vanilla. Beat in flour mixture. Cover dough with plastic wrap and refrigerate 1 hour. Shape dough into 1-inch balls; and place on lightly greased baking sheets. Bake at 375 degrees for 10 to 12 minutes. Remove cookies to wire racks to cool completely. To coat, brush each cookie with melted white chocolate. Sprinkle tops with crushed candy canes. Place on waxed paper to harden.

Yield: 4 dozen puffs.

Peppermint Cherry Delight

6 tablespoons butter
4 ounces chocolate
  graham crackers,
  finely crushed
3 large peppermint
  candy canes, finely
  crushed

1 (8 ounce) package
  cream cheese,
  softened
1 cup powdered sugar
8 large peppermint
  candy canes,
  finely crushed

1 (16 ounce) tub
  whipped topping
1 (21 ounce) can cherry
  pie filling

Melt butter and mix with graham crackers and crushed candy canes.
Press into bottom of 8-inch square pan. Beat together cream cheese,
sugar, and crushed candy canes. Fold cream cheese and whipped
topping together. Spread over graham crackers. Spoon cherry
filling over cheese mixture. Refrigerate until serving time.

Yield: 12 servings.

Peppermint Sundae

1 large scoop vanilla
ice cream
Hot fudge sauce

1 large peppermint candy
cane, finely crushed
Whipped topping

In ice cream bowl or parfait glass, layer ice cream and hot fudge sauce
with crushed candy canes and top with whipped topping.

Yield: 1 sundae.

Peppermint Candy Fudge

2½ cups sugar
½ cup butter
1 (5 ounce) can
  evaporated milk

1 (7 ounce) jar
  marshmallow creme
8 ounces almond
  bark

12 large peppermint
  candy canes, finely
  crushed and divided
1 to 2 drops red food
  coloring

Line 9x13-inch pan with foil so that foil extends over sides of pan. Butter foil. In large saucepan, combine sugar, butter, and milk. Bring to boil, stirring constantly. Remove from heat. Add marshmallow creme and almond bark. Blend until smooth. Stir in peppermint candy canes, reserving 3 tablespoons. Add desired amount of red food coloring. Pour into prepared pan. Cool to room temperature. Score fudge into squares. Put remaining crushed peppermint candy on top of fudge. Refrigerate until firm. Remove fudge from pan by lifting foil. Remove foil from fudge. Using a large knife, cut through scored lines. Store in refrigerator.

Yield: 90 pieces of fudge.

Peppermint Cherry Cordials

1 (18.25 ounce) box
    yellow cake mix
⅓ cup oil
3 eggs
½ cup water

1 (21 ounce) can cherry
    pie filling
½ teaspoon peppermint
    extract

1 (16 ounce) can vanilla
    frosting
2 (10 ounce) bags dark
    chocolate chips

Combine cake mix, oil, eggs, water, pie filling, and extract. Bake according to cake box directions. After cake is cooked, crumble into large bowl. Soften frosting in microwave and gently fold into warm, coarsely crumbled cake. Roll mixture into quarter-sized balls and place on waxed paper–covered cookie sheet. Heat chocolate in microwave, stirring occasionally, until melted and smooth. Using thin-tined fork, dip cake balls into melted chocolate, tapping fork on side of bowl to remove excess chocolate. Place dipped balls on cold, waxed paper–covered cookie sheet and sprinkle with remaining crushed candy canes.

Yield: 40 cordials.

Peppermint Creams

1 cup mashed potatoes (not instant), whipped smooth
1 teaspoon salt
2 tablespoons butter, melted
¾ teaspoon peppermint extract
12 large peppermint candy canes, finely crushed and divided
10 plus cups powdered sugar
16 ounces semisweet chocolate
3 tablespoons shortening

In large bowl, mix together mashed potatoes, salt, butter, peppermint extract, and crushed candy canes (reserving 3 tablespoons). Gradually mix in sugar until you have a workable dough, about 10 cups. Place in freezer for 1 hour. Remove and let dough soften slightly then scoop out small amounts of dough and roll into cherry-sized balls. Place on sheets of waxed paper and flatten. Freeze for 1 hour. In microwave, combine chocolate and shortening, stirring occasionally until melted and smooth. Dip patties in melted chocolate with thin-tined fork. Sprinkle with remaining candy canes and return to freezer for another hour.

Yield: 48 creams.

Peppermint Candies

2 cups powdered sugar
2 tablespoons butter
1 egg white

¼ teaspoon peppermint
    extract
6 candy canes, finely
    crushed and divided

Cream together sugar and butter. Add egg white, extract, and crushed candy canes (reserving 3 tablespoons). Mix well, adding extra sugar, if needed, to make a soft dough. Roll into balls the size of large marbles and press with fork to flatten. Sprinkle remaining crushed candy canes over mints. Allow to harden before serving.

Yield: 60 mints.

Chocolate Pudding Candy Cane Dessert

1½ cups flour
1½ sticks butter
¾ cup walnuts, chopped
4 large peppermint
   candy canes, coarsely
   chopped

8 ounces cream cheese,
   softened
1 cup powdered sugar
1 cup whipped topping
2 (3.9 ounce) packages
   chocolate instant
   pudding mix

3 cups milk, chilled
8 large peppermint
   candy canes, finely
   crushed and divided
Additional whipped
   topping

Combine flour, butter, walnuts, and chopped candy canes. Press into 9 x 13-inch pan. Bake at 350 degrees for 15 minutes. Mix together cream cheese, sugar, and whipped topping. Spread on top of cooled crust. Mix pudding mix, milk, and half the crushed candy canes with electric mixer and spread on top of filling. Top with additional whipped topping and crushed candy canes. Refrigerate.

Yield: 12 servings.

Peppermint Ice

10 ounces white candy coating

8 large candy canes, finely crushed and divided

2 large peppermint candy canes, coarsely chopped

⅛ teaspoon peppermint extract

2 drops red food coloring

Melt white coating in microwave, stirring occasionally, until melted and smooth. Stir in crushed and chopped candy cane pieces (reserving 3 tablespoons), extract, and food coloring, mixing thoroughly. Pour onto cookie sheet lined with waxed paper, garnish with remaining crushed candy canes, and chill. When candy has hardened break into pieces.

Yield: 36 pieces.

Minty Cream Puffs

1½ cups whipping cream
2 tablespoons sugar
1 cup mascarpone
   cheese, softened

4 large peppermint
   candy canes, finely
   crushed

18 pasty puffs, cut in
   half
Powdered sugar
Fresh mint leaves

Whip cream and sugar together. Fold ⅓ of sugar mixture into mascarpone cheese to lighten. Fold in remaining whipped cream mixture. Fold in crushed candy canes. Scrape into piping bag and pipe mixture into bottom halves of puffs. Cover with top halves. Sprinkle puffs with powdered sugar and garnish with mint leaves.

Yield: 18 puffs.

Peppermint Truffles

2 (10 ounce) packages white chocolate chips

½ cup heavy whipping cream

¼ teaspoon peppermint extract

10 large peppermint candy canes, finely crushed

In microwave, melt 1 bag of chips with cream, stirring occasionally, until melted and smooth. Stir in peppermint extract. Pour into shallow pan. Refrigerate 1 to 2 hours or until firm but pliable. Roll into 1-inch balls. In microwave, melt second bag of chips, stirring occasionally, until melted and smooth. Then, using 2 toothpicks to hold balls, dip into chocolate and roll in crushed candy cane. Cool.

Yield: 5 dozen truffles.

Candy Cane Fudge

2 cups sugar
1 teaspoon salt
6 tablespoons unsalted
  butter
1 cup heavy cream

3½ cups mini
  marshmallows
3 cups semisweet or
  white chocolate chips
1 teaspoon vanilla

⅛ teaspoon peppermint
  extract
½ cup crushed pepper-
  mint candy canes

In saucepan over medium heat, combine sugar, salt, butter, cream, and
marshmallows, stirring until butter and marshmallows are almost melted—
5 to 6 minutes. Bring to boil; cook, stirring occasionally, 5 minutes.
Remove from heat. Add chips, vanilla, and peppermint extract. Stir
until chips are melted. Pour mixture into 9 x 13-inch pan lined with
2 long pieces of greased waxed paper with ends overhanging sides
of pan. Sprinkle with candy canes. Let cool in pan about 3 hours.
Use edges of paper to lift out fudge. Place on cutting board
and remove paper. Cut fudge into bars.

Yield: 24 squares of fudge.

Peppermint Bark

12 ounces dark
  chocolate chips
½ teaspoon peppermint
  extract

6 large peppermint
  candy canes,
  coarsely chopped

Melt chocolate in microwave, stirring occasionally, until melted and
smooth. Add peppermint extract and stir. Pour melted chocolate onto
cookie sheet lined with waxed paper and spread with spatula or wooden
spoon. Sprinkle candy cane pieces onto chocolate and gently press
them in with your fingers. Place in freezer for 5 minutes or
until hardened. Break into pieces and serve or place in an
airtight container and refrigerate.

Yield: 36 pieces.

Peppermint Stick Dessert

2 cups vanilla wafer
crumbs
1 (16 ounce) tub
whipped topping

2 cups miniature
marshmallows
⅔ cup pecans, chopped

1 cup peppermint candy
canes, chopped

Butter one 9 x 13-inch dish. Press 1½ cups vanilla wafer crumbs into bottom of dish. Mix together whipped topping, marshmallows, pecans, and ¾ cup crushed candy canes. Sprinkle remaining crumbs on top. Garnish with remaining crushed candy canes. Refrigerate 24 hours or freeze before serving to allow the candy to dissolve.

Yield: 12 servings.

Peppermint Kisses

2 egg whites
⅛ teaspoon salt
⅛ teaspoon cream
  tartar

½ cup white sugar
1 to 2 drops
  peppermint extract

4 peppermint candy
  canes, finely crushed

In large mixing bowl, beat egg whites, salt, and cream of tartar to soft peaks. Gradually add sugar, then extract, continuing to beat until whites form stiff peaks. Drop by teaspoonfuls 1 inch apart on 2 foil-lined cookie sheets. Sprinkle crushed peppermint candy over cookies. Bake at 225 degrees for 1½ hours. Meringues should be completely dry on the inside. Do not allow them to brown. Turn off oven. Keep oven door ajar, and let meringues sit in oven until completely cool. Loosen from foil with metal spatula. Store loosely covered in cool dry place.

Yield: 18 kisses.

Candy Cane Brownie Parfait

1 (19 ounce) package
brownie mix
3 cups peppermint ice
cream, softened

3 cups whipped
topping
7 large peppermint
candy canes, finely
crushed

Prepare brownie mix as directed on package. Pour into greased 9 x 13-inch pan.
Bake at 350 degrees for 28 to 30 minutes. Cool completely. Cut
into squares. Layer brownie, ice cream, whipped topping, and
crushed candy canes in tall glass. Repeat layers to top of glass,
ending with whipped topping and crushed candy canes.

Yield: 12 parfaits.

Peppermint Fudge

2 (10 ounce) packages
vanilla baking chips
1 (14 ounce) can
sweetened condensed
milk

½ teaspoon peppermint
extract
1 dash red or green food
coloring

10 large peppermint
candy canes, finely
crushed

Combine vanilla chips and milk in saucepan over medium heat. Stir frequently until almost melted. Remove from heat and continue to stir until smooth. Stir in peppermint extract, food coloring, and crushed candy canes. Spread evenly in bottom of greased foil-lined, 8-inch square baking pan. Chill for 2 hours and cut into squares.

Yield: 64 pieces of fudge.

Holiday Cream Cheese Fudge

2 ounces cream cheese,
softened
2 cups powdered sugar
3 tablespoons cocoa
1 teaspoon milk

½ teaspoon vanilla
¼ cup nuts, chopped
2 ounces cream cheese,
softened
2 cups powdered sugar
1 teaspoon milk

½ teaspoon peppermint
extract
6 large peppermint
candy canes, finely
crushed

In small mixing bowl, beat 2 ounces cream cheese. Gradually beat in
sugar, cocoa, milk, and vanilla. Stir in nuts. Spread into 9 x 13-inch
cookie sheet that has been lined with foil greased with butter.
Chill 1 hour. Peppermint layer: Beat cream cheese in small
mixing bowl. Gradually beat in sugar, milk, and peppermint
extract. Stir in crushed candy canes. Spread evenly over
chocolate layer. Chill 1 hour. Use foil to lift
fudge from pan. Gently peel off foil.
Cut into squares.

Yield: 8 dozen squares.

Peppermint Caramels

1 cup butter
2¼ cups brown sugar, packed

1 (14 ounce) can sweetened condensed milk
1 cup dark corn syrup

In saucepan over medium heat, melt butter. Add brown sugar, milk, crushed candy canes, and corn syrup. Cook and stir until candy thermometer reads 250 degrees. Pour into greased, foil-lined 9 x 13-inch cookie sheet (do not scrape saucepan). Cool completely before cutting into bite-size pieces.

Yield: 9 dozen caramels.

Peppermint Ice Cream

4 egg yolks	¼ teaspoon salt	1 cup peppermint candy
1½ cups half-and-half	2 cups whipping cream	canes, crushed
¾ cup sugar	4½ teaspoons vanilla	

In heavy saucepan, whisk egg yolks, half-and-half, sugar, and salt. Cook over low heat, stirring constantly, until mixture reaches 160 degrees and coats back of metal spoon. Remove from heat. Place pan in bowl of ice water and stir for 2 minutes. Stir in whipping cream and vanilla. Press plastic wrap onto surface of custard. Refrigerate for several hours. Fill cylinder of ice cream freezer ⅔ full. (Refrigerate any remaining mixture until ready to freeze.) Freeze according to manufacturer's directions. Stir in crushed candy canes. Allow to ripen in ice cream freezer or firm up in refrigerator freezer for 2 to 4 hours before serving.

Yield: 8 servings.

White Candy Cane Fudge

12 ounces white chocolate chips
1 (14 ounce) can sweetened condensed milk

6 large peppermint candy canes, coarsely chopped

Over medium heat in top of double-boiler combine white chocolate chips and milk. Cook, stirring frequently, until melted and smooth, about 5 minutes. Pour mixture into 8-inch square buttered baking pan with sides lined with buttered foil to extend over sides of pan by 1 inch. Sprinkle candy over top. Using a knife lightly swirl candy into chocolate mixture. Refrigerate until firm, about 6 hours. Cut into 1-inch squares. Store in refrigerator.

Yield: 64 pieces.

Beverages

The coming of Christ by way of a Bethlehem manger seems
strange and stunning. But when we take Him out of the manger
and invite Him into our hearts, then the meaning
unfolds and the strangeness vanishes.

NEIL C. STRAIT

Chocolate Cheesecake Milkshake

½ ounce package cream
  cheese, softened
4 large peppermint
  candy canes, finely
  crushed and divided

2 cups milk
6 scoops chocolate ice cream
1 cup whipping cream,
  whipped

Place cream cheese, crushed candy canes, and 1 cup milk in blender. Blend until smooth. Place remaining milk and ice cream in blender. Continue to blend until smooth. Pour into glasses and top with whipped cream and reserved crushed candy canes.

Yield: 4 milkshakes.

114

Chocolate Cherry Milkshake

4 scoops vanilla ice
cream or frozen
yogurt
1 cup milk, chilled

¼ cup chocolate syrup
4 maraschino cherries,
stems removed and
divided

2 large peppermint
candy canes, finely
crushed and divided
1 cup whipping cream,
whipped

Place ice cream, milk, syrup, cherries, and crushed candy canes in blender.
Blend until smooth. Pour into glass and top
with whipped topping, cherry, and crushed candy canes.

Yield: 2 milkshakes.

Chocolate Chip Peppermint Milkshake

1 milk chocolate candy bar, chopped
2 large peppermint candy canes, finely crushed
2 cups milk
3 tablespoons chocolate syrup
2 to 3 scoops vanilla ice cream

Put chopped candy bars, crushed candy canes, syrup, ice cream, and milk into blender. Blend for about 3 minutes or until smooth.

Yield: 4 milkshakes.

Peppermint Hot Cocoa Mix

6½ cups powdered milk
1 (5 ounce) package
 chocolate pudding
 cook and serve mix
1 cup powdered choco-
 late drink mix

½ cup powdered
 non-dairy creamer
½ cup powdered sugar
½ cup unsweetened
 cocoa powder

12 large peppermint
 candy canes, finely
 crushed

In large bowl, combine powdered milk, chocolate pudding mix, chocolate drink mix powder, creamer, powdered sugar, cocoa, and crushed candy canes. Dissolve ⅓ cup cocoa mix in 1 cup boiling water.

Yield: 24 servings.

Peppermint Candy Bar Shake

½ cup milk
1 cup vanilla or
   chocolate ice cream

1 large candy bar,
   chopped and
   divided

1 large peppermint
   candy cane, finely
   crushed and divided

Place milk and ice cream into blender and mix until smooth. Pour into glass and sprinkle with reserved candy bar and crushed candy cane.

Yield: 1 shake.

Christmas Espresso

1½ cups espresso beans, finely ground	6 large peppermint candy canes, finely crushed	4 cups milk
3 cups boiling water		4 ounces bittersweet chocolate, chopped
2 tablespoons sugar	1 vanilla bean, split	Whipped cream

Put espresso and water in coffee maker and brew. Combine sugar and crushed candy canes. Set aside. Scrape seeds from vanilla bean into medium saucepan. Add milk and scald over moderate heat, about 5 minutes. Remove from heat, add chocolate, and stir until melted. Cover and keep warm over very low heat. Divide hot espresso into cups. In blender, whip half of warm chocolate milk at low speed. Gradually increase speed to high and blend until frothy, about 1 minute. Pour chocolate milk into cups. Top with whipped cream and crushed candy canes.

Yield: 4 servings.

Peppermint Eggnog Punch

1 quart peppermint
  ice cream
1 quart eggnog

4 (12 ounce) cans
  ginger ale,
  chilled

4 large peppermint
  candy canes, finely
  crushed
8 miniature candy canes

Set aside 2 or 3 round scoops of ice cream in freezer for garnish.
Stir remaining ice cream until softened. Gradually stir in eggnog.
Transfer to punch bowl, and stir in ginger ale. Hang miniature candy
canes around edge of punchbowl. Float reserved ice cream scoops on top.
Sprinkle with crushed candy canes and serve immediately.

Yield: 16 servings.

Snowflake Cocoa

2 cups whipping cream
6 cups milk
1 teaspoon vanilla

1 (12 ounce) package
white chocolate chips
Whipped cream

4 large peppermint
candy canes, finely
crushed

Stir together cream, milk, vanilla, and white chocolate chips in slow cooker. Cover and cook on low, stirring occasionally, until mixture is hot and chocolate chips are melted. Stir again before serving. Garnish with whipped cream and crushed candy canes, as desired.

Yield: 10 servings.

Chocolate Mint Chai Tea

1 bag black tea	2 large candy canes,	1 teaspoon allspice
½ cup boiling water	finely crushed	½ teaspoon cardamom,
3 tablespoons sugar	2 cups milk	finely ground
2 tablespoons cocoa	1 teaspoon vanilla	
powder		

In small saucepan, pour boiling water over tea bag. Cover and let stand for
3 to 5 minutes. Remove tea bag. Stir in sugar, cocoa, and crushed candy
canes. Cook and stir over medium heat until mixture comes to boil.
Stir in milk, vanilla, and spices. Heat thoroughly. Do not boil.
Pour into mugs.

Yield: 4 servings.

Candy Cane Cooler

3 scoops vanilla, or chocolate, ice cream	1½ cups milk	2 large peppermint candy canes, crushed

In blender combine ice cream, milk, and crushed candy canes.
Process until smooth. Pour into mugs.

Yield: 2 servings.

Peppermint Punch

2 quarts peppermint ice cream	2 liters ginger ale, chilled
1 cup milk, chilled	8 large peppermint candy canes, crushed

Place ice cream in punch bowl and allow to soften slightly. Blend in milk
and ginger ale. Stir until frothy. Serve at once, or keep chilled until
ready to serve. Top with crushed candy canes just before serving.

Yield: 24 servings.

Pepper-Minty Iced Coffee

6 ounces freshly brewed coffee	1 scoop peppermint ice cream	1 small candy cane

Pour coffee into large mug and add ice cream. Stir until slightly melted. Garnish with small candy cane stirrer.

Yield: 1 serving.

Christmas Float

1 can cola	Red and green candy-coated chocolate candies, chopped	2 large peppermint candy canes, finely crushed
3 scoops vanilla ice cream		
4 cherries		Whipped topping

In a glass, pour cola over ice cream. Top with whipped topping, cherries, chocolate candies, and crushed candy canes.

Yield: 1 float.

Peppermint Patty's Cocoa

10 chocolate sand-
wich cookies, coarsely
chopped

4 cups milk
½ cup chocolate syrup
¼ teaspoon peppermint
extract

4 peppermint candy
canes, finely crushed

Place all ingredients in blender; cover and blend on high speed
until well blended. Pour into 2-quart saucepan. Cook on
medium-high heat until heated through, stirring frequently.

Yield: 4 servings.

Minty Mocha Cocoa

4 cups milk
1 tablespoon cocoa
¼ cup chocolate syrup
2 tablespoons brown
 sugar

1 tablespoon ground
 coffee
1 teaspoon vanilla
4 peppermint candy
 canes, finely crushed

Small peppermint
 candy canes

Heat milk, cocoa, syrup, sugar, coffee, vanilla, and crushed candy canes in small saucepan and whisk until steaming. Strain and pour into 2 mugs. Serve each with a small candy cane stir stick.

Yield: 4 servings.

Chocolate Mint Espresso

4 cups milk
6 ounces dark baking
chocolate, chopped
3 tablespoons brown
sugar

¾ teaspoon instant
espresso powder
1 teaspoon vanilla

4 large peppermint
candy canes, finely
crushed
4 small peppermint
candy canes

In large saucepan, stir milk over medium heat until heated through.
Remove from heat and add chocolate, brown sugar, espresso
powder, vanilla, and crushed candy canes, stirring until smooth.
Return to heat. Cook and stir until heated thoroughly. Pour
into mugs and serve with small candy canes as stir sticks.

Yield: 4 servings.

Peppermint Twist Cocoa

4 cups milk
3 ounces white
   chocolate, chopped

5 large peppermint
   candy canes, finely
   crushed and divided

Whipped topping

Bring milk to a simmer in saucepan. Reduce heat to medium-low. Add
white chocolate and all but 2 tablespoons of crushed candy canes.
Whisk until smooth. Serve with whipped topping and sprinkle
with remaining crushed candy canes.

Yield: 4 servings.

Choco-Mint Cocoa

½ cup sugar
¼ cup instant cocoa mix
3 ounces dark chocolate chips
⅓ cup hot water

4 cups milk
1 teaspoon vanilla
¼ teaspoon peppermint extract

4 large peppermint candy canes, finely crushed

Mix sugar, cocoa mix, chocolate chips, and hot water in saucepan over medium heat; stirring continually until chocolate chips are melted. Add milk, vanilla, peppermint extract, and crushed candy canes. Continue to stir until hot.

Yield: 4 servings.

Chocolate Mint Hot Chocolate

4 cups chocolate milk
6 chocolate creme mints, chopped

4 large peppermint candy canes, finely crushed

Mini marshmallows
4 small candy canes

In medium saucepan over medium-low heat, combine milk, chopped chocolate mints, and crushed candy canes. Stir until chocolate is melted. Pour into mugs and top with mini marshmallows and a small candy cane for stirring.

Yield: 4 servings.

Double Chocolate Mint Cocoa Mix

6 cups nonfat milk
powder
1 (16 ounce) package
powdered sugar

2 (8 ounce) jars
chocolate-flavored
nondairy powdered
creamer

8 large peppermint
candy canes, finely
crushed
¼ cup cocoa powder

Process milk powder, 2 cups at a time, in blender or food processor.
Combine all ingredients in large bowl. To serve, pour 6 ounces boiling
water over 3 tablespoons cocoa mix. Stir until well blended.
Store mix in airtight container in refrigerator.

Yield: 24 servings.

Minty Eggnog

½ gallon vanilla ice cream

2 quarts eggnog, chilled

2 liters lemon-lime flavored carbonated beverage

10 large peppermint candy canes, finely crushed

1 cup heavy whipping cream, whipped

10 chocolate mint candies, coarsely chopped

In large punch bowl, combine ice cream, eggnog, carbonated beverage, and finely crushed candy canes. Mix well. Place dollops of whipped cream on top and sprinkle with coarsely chopped chocolate mint candies for garnish.

Yield: 48 servings.

Christmas Wassail

1 gallon apple cider
1 teaspoon ground
  cloves
1 teaspoon ground
  allspice
1 teaspoon ground
  nutmeg

1 teaspoon ground
  cinnamon
1 (6 ounce) can frozen
  lemonade, thawed
1 (6 ounce) can frozen
  orange juice, thawed

½ cup firmly packed
  brown sugar
8 large peppermint
  candy canes, finely
  crushed

Combine 2 cups apple cider and spices in large kettle or pot.
Bring to a boil. Reduce heat and simmer for 10 minutes.
Add remaining cider, lemonade, orange juice, sugar,
and crushed candy canes. Heat until hot.
Do not boil.

Yield: 45 servings.

Slush Punch

2½ cups sugar
6 cups water
2 (3 ounce) packages strawberry-flavored gelatin

8 large peppermint candy canes, finely crushed
1 (46 ounce) can pineapple juice

⅔ cup lemon juice
1 quart orange juice
2 (2 liter) bottles lemon-lime flavored carbonated beverage

In large saucepan, combine sugar, water, gelatin, and crushed candy canes. Boil for 3 minutes. Stir in pineapple juice, lemon juice, and orange juice. Divide mixture in half. Freeze in 2 separate containers. When ready to serve, place frozen contents of one container in punch bowl, and stir in 1 bottle lemon-lime beverage until slushy. When needed, repeat with second container and second bottle of lemon-lime beverage.

Almond Milk Peppermint Latte

2 cups vanilla-flavored almond milk

2 large peppermint candy canes, finely crushed and divided

1 cup instant espresso-style coffee
Pinch cocoa

Warm milk and crushed candy canes in saucepan or in microwave. Pour into blender and whip until milk becomes a dense foam. Prepare espresso-style coffee according to package instructions, filling each mug halfway. Pour milk into mugs. Dust each mug with a pinch of cocoa and reserved crushed candy canes.

Yield: 2 servings.

Creamy Candy Cane Hot Chocolate

1 (14 ounce) can sweetened condensed milk
½ cup unsweetened cocoa
1½ teaspoons vanilla
⅛ teaspoon salt
8 large peppermint candy canes, finely crushed and divided
6½ cups hot water
Whipped cream

In large saucepan over medium heat, combine milk, cocoa, vanilla, salt, and crushed candy canes. Mix well. Slowly stir in hot water. Heat completely, stirring occasionally. Do not boil. Wet rim of each cup and press into reserved candy canes. Top with whipped cream.

Yield: 8 servings.

General Yumminess

When they were come into the house, they saw the young child
with Mary his mother, and fell down, and worshipped him:
and when they had opened their treasures, they presented unto him gifts;
gold, and frankincense and myrrh.

MATTHEW 2:11

Chocolate Mint Apple Dip

1 (14 ounce) can sweet-
    ened condensed milk
1 cup semisweet
    chocolate chips

10 chocolate-covered
    peppermint patties,
    chopped

8 large peppermint
    candy canes, finely
    crushed and divided
Sliced apples

In small saucepan, combine milk, chocolate chips, peppermint patties, and half the crushed candy canes. Cook and stir over medium-low heat until smooth. Serve warm with apples. Sprinkle dipped apple slices with remaining crushed candy canes before eating.

Yield: 2½ cups.

Candy Cane Popcorn

| ½ cup unpopped popcorn | 4 ounces white chocolate candy coating | 12 large peppermint candy canes, coarsely chopped |

Place popped popcorn in large bowl, and discard unpopped kernels. Melt candy coating according to package directions. Pour melted coating over popcorn, and sprinkle chopped candy canes over mixture. Using your hands, work candy coating and crushed candy canes all through popcorn. Let mixture cool. Break into bite-size pieces.

Yield: 40 servings.

Marshmallow Mint Frosting

2 egg whites, unbeaten
1½ cups sugar
6 tablespoons water
8 large peppermint
   candy canes, finely
   crushed and divided

6 large marshmallows,
   quartered
¼ teaspoon peppermint
   extract
¼ teaspoon cream of
   tartar

In double boiler, over boiling water, combine egg whites, sugar, water, crushed candy canes (reserving 3 tablespoons), and quartered marshmallows. Continuing over rapidly boiling water, beat for about 10 minutes or until mixture stands in peaks. (Use portable electric mixer). Remove top of double boiler from heat and stir in extract and cream of tartar. Beat for another 5 minutes or until good spreading consistency is reached. Cool before using. Remaining crushed candy canes can be sprinkled over icing.

Yield: Enough for 1 cake.

Peppermint Frosting

1½ cups powdered sugar
3 tablespoons whipping cream, approximately

1 teaspoon vanilla
¼ teaspoon peppermint extract

6 large peppermint candy canes, finely crushed

Add enough cream to sugar to make a spreadable consistency.

Add vanilla, peppermint, and crushed candy canes.

Mix thoroughly.

Yield: Enough for 1 cake.

Peppermint Syrup

1 cup of sugar	8 large peppermint
1 cup of water	candy canes,
	finely crushed

Combine sugar, water, and crushed candy canes in saucepan. Using candy thermometer, boil until mixture reaches 225 degrees, stirring constantly. Keep syrup on medium-low heat until all candy is dissolved. Then increase to medium heat. Drizzle over ice cream and cakes or add to hot or cold drinks.

Yield: 1 cup.

Chocolate Peppermint Frosting

1¼ cups skim milk
1 (3.9 ounce) package
chocolate flavor
instant pudding mix

10 large peppermint
candy canes, finely
crushed

2 (1.3 ounce) envelopes
whipped dessert
topping mix

Place milk in large bowl. Add pudding mix, crushed candy canes, and topping mix. Beat at low speed until dry bits are gone. Beat at high speed 2 to 3 minutes or until stiff, scraping sides and bottom of bowl constantly.

Yield: Enough for 1 cake.

Little Cookie Houses

1 (16 ounce) container
   vanilla icing
6 large peppermint
   candy canes, finely
   crushed

Assorted large crackers
   and cookies for
   building
Sugar wafers and round,
   scalloped butter
   cookies

Assorted decorations
   and colorful candies,
   including candy canes,
   pretzel sticks, ice
   cream cones, gum
   drops, candy-coated
   chocolate pieces,
   wafer candies, etc.

Combine icing and crushed candy canes until mixed thoroughly. Spread frosting on large cracker or cookie edges. Hold edges together for a few minutes until set. Decorate as desired. For log cabin, ice outer walls and attach pretzel sticks. For church, make steeple from iced sugar wafer, with pretzel cross on top. Decorate roofs with finely crushed candy canes immediately after icing to add an icy sheen. Use wafer candies as shingles, by spreading roof with frosting, then layering rows from the bottom up.

Yield: 1 to 2 little houses.

Creamy Christmas Icing

1 (16 ounce) container vanilla or chocolate icing	¼ teaspoon peppermint extract	8 peppermint candy canes, finely crushed and divided

In medium bowl, mix icing, extract, and crushed candy canes (reserving 3 tablespoons), until well blended. After icing cake, sprinkle remaining crushed candy canes over top of cake.

Yield: Enough for 1 cake.

Peppermint Eggnog Pudding

1 (5.1 ounce) package
vanilla instant
pudding mix

6 large peppermint
candy canes, finely
crushed
4 dashes ground
cinnamon

2 dashes ground nutmeg
Pinch ground ginger
1 cup milk, chilled
2 cups eggnog

Mix dry pudding in bowl with crushed candy canes and spices until
well blended. Whisk in milk and eggnog, stirring 2 minutes, or until no
lumps remain. Pour pudding into serving dishes and refrigerate
2 hours or until set.

Yield: 6 servings.

Minty Marshmallow Salad

1 (15 ounce) can
crushed pineapple,
with juice
8 large peppermint
candy canes,
finely crushed

1 (3 ounce) package
strawberry flavored
gelatin
2 cups whipping cream,
whipped

1 (10.5 ounce) package
miniature
marshmallows

Pour pineapple with juice and crushed candy canes into mixing bowl.
Sprinkle in gelatin and stir until dissolved. Refrigerate 1 to 2 hours until
set. Fold in whipped cream and marshmallows. Pour into tube pan or
gelatin mold and freeze until nearly solid, about 1 hour.
Unmold gelatin and cut into 12 pieces. Serve partially frozen.

Yield: 12 servings.

Peppermint Candied Apples

15 apples
15 craft sticks
2 cups white sugar
1 cup light corn syrup

12 large peppermint
candy canes, finely
crushed
1½ cups water

4 drops red food
coloring

Insert craft sticks into whole, stemmed apples. In medium saucepan over medium-high heat, combine sugar, corn syrup, crushed candy canes, and water. Heat to 300 degrees, without stirring, or until small amount of syrup dropped into cold water forms hard, brittle threads. Remove from heat and stir in food coloring. Place pan in hot water while dipping apples to keep candy coating soft. Holding apple by its stick, dip in syrup and remove and turn to coat evenly. Place on lightly greased cookie sheets to harden.

Yield: 15 apples.

Christmas Mocha Icing

½ stick butter, softened
2 teaspoons instant
  coffee

2 tablespoons unsweet-
  ened cocoa
6 large peppermint
  candy canes, finely
  crushed

3 cups powdered sugar
1½ teaspoons vanilla
3 tablespoons milk

Cream butter, coffee, cocoa, and crushed candy canes until smooth.
Slowly add sugar, vanilla, and milk. Beat until smooth and spreadable.

Yield: Enough for 1 cake.

Holiday Popcorn Mix

9 cups corn cereal
  squares
4 cups popped popcorn
1½ cups almonds
1 cup brown sugar,
  packed

½ cup butter
½ cup corn syrup
8 large peppermint
  candy canes, finely
  crushed
1 teaspoon vanilla

½ teaspoon baking soda
2 cups chocolate chips
6 ounces sweetened
  dried cranberries

Grease cookie sheet with sides. Mix cereal, popcorn, and almonds in pan.
Combine sugar, butter, corn syrup, and crushed candy canes in saucepan.
Bring to boil over medium heat, stirring constantly. Remove from heat.
Stir in vanilla and baking soda. Pour evenly over cereal mixture and stir to
coat evenly. Bake at 250 degrees for 45 minutes stirring every 15 minutes.
Cool completely in pan, stirring frequently to
break apart mixture. Stir in chocolate chips
and cranberries.

Yield: 36 servings.

Chocolate Mint Fondue

1 (10 ounce) bag chocolate chips
1 drop peppermint extract

1 (16 ounce) bag large marshmallows
1 store bought sponge cake, cut into 1-inch squares

6 large peppermint candy canes, finely crushed
6 large peppermint candy canes

Melt chocolate and add extract. Mix well. Using candy canes as dipping sticks, dip marshmallows and sponge cake pieces into melted chocolate then sprinkle with crushed candy canes.

Yield: 30 servings.

151

Chocolate Peppermint Pretzels

6 ounces white chocolate chips	1 (15 ounce) package mini-twist pretzels	8 large peppermint candy canes, finely crushed
1½ teaspoons shortening		

Melt white chocolate in double boiler, stirring constantly. Dip each pretzel into white chocolate, completely covering half the pretzel. Roll in crushed candy cane, and lay on waxed paper.

Place in refrigerator for 15 minutes to harden.

Store in airtight container.

Yield: 16 servings.

Minty Marshmallow Frosting

2 egg whites, unbeaten
1½ cups sugar
6 large peppermint
candy canes, finely
crushed

6 tablespoons water
6 large marshmallows,
quartered
½ teaspoon peppermint
extract

½ teaspoon vanilla
¼ teaspoon cream of
tartar

In double boiler, over boiling water, combine egg whites, sugar, crushed candy canes, water, and quartered marshmallows. Cook over rapidly boiling water, beating for about 10 minutes or until mixture stands in peaks. Remove from heat and stir in peppermint, vanilla, and cream of tartar. Beat for another 5 minutes or until a good spreading consistency is reached.

Yield: Enough for 1 cake.

Candy Cane Pudding Mugs

1 (5 ounce) package
  white chocolate cook
  and serve pudding

3 cups milk
⅔ cup miniature
  marshmallows

8 large peppermint
  candy canes, finely
  crushed and divided

Mix pudding and milk in medium saucepan. Bring to full boil on medium heat, stirring constantly. Remove from heat. Stir in marshmallows and sprinkle with crushed candy canes.

Yield: 6 servings.

Candy Cane Caramel Apples

6 green apples
6 wooden sticks
1 (14 ounce) package
individually wrapped
caramels, unwrapped

2 tablespoons water
6 large peppermint
candy canes, finely
crushed
½ teaspoon vanilla

2 large peppermint
candy canes, finely
crushed

Insert wooden sticks ¾ of the way into stem end of each apple. Place apples on cookie sheet covered with lightly greased aluminum foil. Combine caramels, water, and 6 crushed candy canes in saucepan over low heat. Stir often, until caramel melts and is smooth. Stir in vanilla. Dip each apple into caramel and gently run apples around insides of saucepan. Scrape excess caramel from apple bottoms using side of saucepan. Sprinkle dipped apples with remaining crushed candy canes. Place on aluminum foil and chill until ready to serve.

Yield: 6 apples.

Peppermint Glaze

1 cup powdered sugar
¼ teaspoon peppermint
extract

4 large peppermint
candy canes, finely
crushed

2 tablespoons cream

In small bowl, mix together sugar, extract, and crushed candy canes, and
cream until smooth. Add cream by ½ teaspoonfuls if glaze
is too thick to spread.

Candied Marshmallows

1 cup powdered sugar
5 teaspoons water
1 (16 ounce) package
    jumbo marshmallows

8 large peppermint
    candy canes, finely
    crushed
Toothpicks

Pour powdered sugar into bowl. Add water 1 teaspoon at a time until you've created a thin glaze. Place toothpick in end of marshmallow. Roll marshmallow in glaze, covering bottom and sides. Roll marshmallow in crushed candy canes until glaze is covered. Place on cookie sheet lined with waxed paper and put in freezer. They are done when marshmallow pops off easily from waxed paper. Store leftovers in bag in freezer.

Yield: 30 marshmallows.

Notes

Notes

Notes

Notes

Notes

Notes

Notes

Notes

Recipe Index